Powerful Predators

SHARKS
OCEAN HUNTERS

Norman Pearl

PowerKiDS
press™

New York

Published in 2009 by The Rosen Publishing Group, Inc.
29 East 21st Street, New York, NY 10010

First Edition

Editor: Amelie von Zumbusch
Book Design: Julio Gil
Photo Researcher: Jessica Gerweck

Photo Credits: Cover © Stephen Frink/Getty Images; pp. 5, 7, 9, 15, 19 Shutterstock.com; p. 11 © Jeff Rotman/Getty Images; p. 13 © Jeffrey L. Rotman/Peter Arnold, Inc.; p. 17 © Brian J. Skerry/Getty Images; p. 21 © iStockphoto.com/Chuck Babbitt; back cover (top to bottom) Shutterstock.com, Shutterstock.com, © Kim Wolhuter/Getty Images, Shutterstock.com, © Stephen Frink/Getty Images, Shutterstock.com.

Library of Congress Cataloging-in-Publication Data

Pearl, Norman.
  Sharks : ocean hunters / Norman Pearl. — 1st ed.
      p. cm. — (Powerful predators)
  Includes index.
  ISBN 978-1-4042-4509-9 (library binding)
  1. Sharks—Juvenile literature. I. Title.
  QL638.9.P425 2009
  597.3—dc22
                                    2008006842

Manufactured in the United States of America

Contents

Shark!

Shark! That very word scares people. Almost everyone has heard stories about terrible shark **attacks** that left the water bloody. Many people think of sharks as monsters in the water that are up to no good. However, while a few shark attacks take place each year, most sharks would never attack a person.

In most ways, sharks are like all other fish. Sharks have lived in the world's seas for 400 **million** years. Even before there were dinosaurs, there were sharks! It looks like sharks are here to stay, so we should try to understand and not just fear them.

As all fish do, sharks have gills, or a row of thin openings, on their sides. Sharks and other fish breathe through their gills.

Are They All Sharks?

One thing many people do not know about sharks is that there are many kinds of sharks. No one is sure exactly how many sorts of sharks there are because new ones are still being found. Today there are about 375 known types of sharks.

Sharks do not all look alike. The largest known shark is the whale shark. The biggest whale shark on record was more than 60 feet (18 m) long and weighed 90,000 pounds (40,823 kg). Other sharks, such as the spined pygmy shark, are as small as 6 inches (15 cm) long. That is shorter than a new pencil!

Zebra sharks live in the Indian Ocean and Pacific Ocean.
These sharks often have fish called remoras sticking to them.

Bathing Beauties

No matter what size a shark is, its **skeleton** is made of cartilage. Cartilage is bendable matter that is not as hard as the bones that make up a person's skeleton. All sharks also have openings in their sides, called gills. Sharks use gills to breathe in the water.

Many people think that all sharks are gray. However, some sharks have colorful stripes and spots. Some sharks, such as lantern sharks, even have body parts that glow in the dark ocean. Sharks' eyes come in many colors, as well. Some sharks have black eyes, while others have green, gold, or silvery gray eyes.

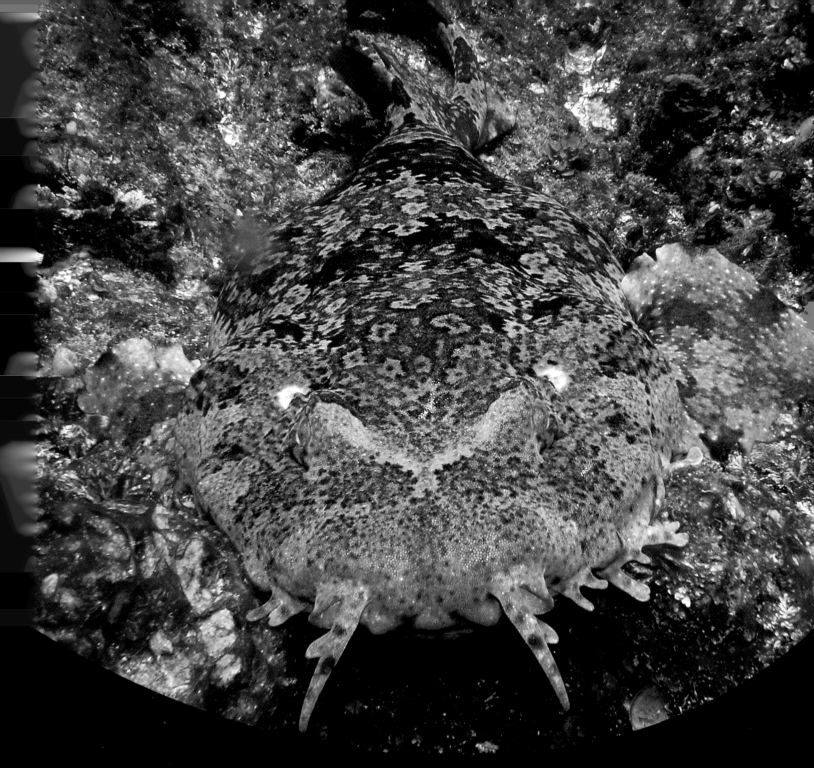

Wobbegongs have spotted skin that makes these sharks hard to see against the seafloor, where they spend most of their time.

A Mouth Built for Biting

Many sharks have strong **jaws** to help them catch **prey**. A shark's jaws can come apart so that the shark can push its whole mouth forward. This lets the shark's teeth firmly lock on to its supper in the sea.

Many sharks have jaws that hold several rows of sharp teeth. Different sharks have different types of teeth. Some have pointed teeth, while others have teeth with sharp edges. Even though a shark may have hundreds of teeth, it will never need a dentist. When a shark's teeth become worn or broken, they fall out. This makes room for new teeth to grow in.

A shark's many rows of sharp teeth make it a very powerful predator, or hunter.

Here Come the Shark Pups

Most shark babies already have full sets of teeth when they are born. Baby sharks are called pups. Shark pups can be born in several ways. After some kinds of **male** and **female** sharks **mate**, the female gives birth to live babies. However, other kinds of sharks lay eggs. In time, pups break out of these eggs.

Shark parents can produce between 2 and 135 young at one time. Once these shark pups are born, they are on their own. Shark mothers do not stay around to care for their young, and many shark pups are eaten by bigger sharks.

Baby sharks, such as this baby sand shark, have yolk sacs that supply them with food.

You can find sharks in every ocean of the world. Some live in deep waters near the ocean floor, while others are found near the ocean's **surface**. Most sharks live in warm waters, but some types can be found in icy **polar** seas.

Even though most sharks are saltwater, or ocean, fish, a few can also live in freshwater. These sharks have been known to swim up rivers. For example, large sharks called bull sharks have been seen in the Mississippi River. One was even spotted in Illinois, 1,800 miles (2,897 km) up the river from the ocean!

This whitetip reef shark is swimming in the warm waters around Hawaii. Whitetip reef sharks live in the Indian Ocean and Pacific Ocean.

Great Hunters

Sharks are great hunters! Some sharks can hear a fish more than 700 feet (213 m) from them. Other sharks can smell prey 1 mile (2 km) away!

Different kinds of sharks attack their prey differently. Some sharks use surprise in their attacks. These sharks swim quietly toward their prey and strike from below. Other sharks circle their prey before striking. Certain sharks even bump into their prey before they attack it. Some sharks hunt in packs and share the prey. These sharks often herd a group of fish into **shallow** water and attack them there.

Oceanic whitetip sharks eat mostly squid, octopuses, and fish.
Sometimes these sharks even follow schools, or groups, of fish around.

Hammerhead sharks use sense **organs** in their wide, flat noses to find prey. Many people fear these skilled hunters. However, most of the nine kinds of hammerheads are not **dangerous**. Some people even enjoy swimming with hammerheads!

The only danger comes from the great hammerhead shark. This largest member of the hammerhead family is one of the world's biggest meat-eating fish. It can grow up to 20 feet (6 m) long and weigh 1,000 pounds (454 kg). Like many large sharks, it attacks large prey. It is not a good idea to get close to one of these sharks, as it might mistake you for its food.

Hammerhead sharks get their name from their strangely shaped heads.

The Great White Wonder

Another large and powerful shark that people often fear is the great white shark. Most great whites grow to be about 15 feet (5 m) long. These sharks prey on seals, sea lions, dolphins, and other sharks. At times, they have also attacked people. However, these sharks may have attacked by mistake. A person lying on a surfboard can look like a sea lion to a great white.

It is unlikely that a shark will ever attack you. Though you hear a lot about them, such attacks are few in number. People kill sharks much more often than sharks kill people.

Great white sharks are the top predators in the waters where they live. These sharks prey on many animals, but no animals prey on them.

Staying Safe in the Water

Even though shark attacks are uncommon, you should still be careful in the water. It is a good idea to always swim with others. Sharks are more likely to attack someone who is alone. Also, stay out of the water at sunrise and sunset, when sharks are most active.

Do not go in the water if you have a cut. A shark can smell blood from far away. Leave your shiny **jewelry** at home, too. Jewelry can look like fish scales to a shark. With a little bit of extra care, people and sharks can safely share the world's waters.

Glossary

attacks (uh-TAKS) Acts of trying to hurt someone or something.

dangerous (DAYN-jeh-rus) Might cause hurt.

female (FEE-mayl) Having to do with women and girls.

jaws (JAHZ) Bones in the top and bottom of the mouth.

jewelry (JOO-ul-ree) Objects worn on the body that are made of special metals, such as gold and silver, and valued stones.

male (MAYL) Having to do with men and boys.

mate (MAYT) To come together to make babies.

million (MIL-yun) One thousand thousands.

organs (OR-genz) Parts inside the body that do a job.

polar (POH-lur) Having to do with the areas around the North Pole and the South Pole.

prey (PRAY) An animal that is hunted by another animal for food.

shallow (SHA-loh) Not deep.

skeleton (SKEH-leh-tun) What gives an animal's or a person's body shape.

surface (SER-fes) The outside of anything.

Index

A
attacks, 4, 16, 20, 22

B
babies, 12

D
dinosaurs, 4

F
fish, 4, 16, 18

J
jaws, 10

jewelry, 22

M
monsters, 4

P
people, 4, 8, 18, 20, 22

prey, 10, 16, 18

R
record, 6

S
sea(s), 4, 10, 14

sense organs, 18

skeleton, 8

surface, 14

W
whale shark, 6

Web Sites

Due to the changing nature of Internet links, PowerKids Press has developed an online list of Web sites related to the subject of this book. This site is updated regularly. Please use this link to access the list:

www.powerkidslinks.com/pred/sharks/